بِسْمِ ٱللَّهِ ٱلرَّحْمَٰنِ ٱلرَّحِيمِ

In the name of Allah (swt), the Kind, the Merciful.

Created by Sabilla Karnib
Wisdom Writers 1 Ages 6 - 8
Second edition, 2024.

- a_touch.of_faith
- atouchoffaith.com.au
- atouchoffaith313@gmail.com

Follow our instagram to support and stay up to date with new releases, behind the scenes content and much more!

Thank you for your kind support in helping bring 'Wisdom Writers' to the community and beyond.

# Note for Teachers and Parents

In the name of God, the Kind, the Merciful.
Asalamu Alaykum,

A touch of faith is a small business focused on implementing a touch of faith in the everyday lives of families.

This handwriting book Includes images, colouring, drawing, poetry, activities, Quran verses, hadiths, quotes and sentences that aim to develop and nurture:

- A child's love for God
- A child's love for God's messengers and the 14 infallibles
- A love for nature
- Good character morals and ethics
- Affirmations
- Gratitude
- Creativity
- And Faith

Implementing a touch of faith in a child's everyday life can plant the seed of unconditional love and unwavering faith, towards our creator the Most Merciful.

This handwriting book contains 104 lessons, which is around 3-4 lessons per week for a normal school year and is targeted towards children ages 6 - 8.

Perfect for children with some handwriting experience but are still working on the correct handwriting formation, size and spacing for both letters and numbers. The text size starts out large and gets smaller as the lessons progress.

Every sixth lesson is focused on one of the 14 infallibles, and every seventh lesson is focused on a verse from the Holy Quran.

Each lesson in this handwriting book provides an opportunity for the child to draw, colour, or complete an activity such as a dot-to-do in order to improve fine motor skills, improve drawing skills, enhance their creativity and have fun!

We hope you enjoy every lesson.
Thank you for your support!
God Bless
 - A Touch of Faith

**Abbreviations:**

(pbuh) - May peace be upon him.

(as) - *Alayhis Salaam* - May peace be upon him.

(sa) - *Salaamullah Alayha* - May peace be upon her.

(ajtfs) - *Ajjallahu ta'aala fashajahush shareef* - May God hasten his reappearance.

*Dua Before Studying*

# My Lord! Increase me in my knowledge

# The 14 Infallibles Contents Page

Lesson 6 - The 12 Imams .................................................. Page 15

Lesson 12 - Prophet Muhammad (pbuh).................... Page 27

Lesson 18 - Lady Fatima (sa) ...................................... Page 39

Lesson 24 - Imam Ali (as) ............................................ Page 53

Lesson 30 - Imam Hasan (as)...................................... Page 65

Lesson 36 - Imam Husain (as) .................................... Page 77

Lesson 42 - Imam Ali Zain al Abideen (as) ............... Page 89

Lesson 48 - Imam Muhammad al Baqir (as) ............ Page 101

Lesson 54 - Imam Jafar al Sadiq (as) ........................ Page 113

Lesson 60 - Imam Musa al Kadhim (as) ................... Page 125

Lesson 66 - Imam Ali al Rida (as) .............................. Page 137

Lesson 72 - Imam Muhammad al Taqi (as) .............. Page 149

Lesson 78 - Imam Ali al Hadi (as) .............................. Page 161

Lesson 85 - Imam Hasan al Askari (as) .................... Page 175

Lesson 90 - Imam Mahdi (as) ..................................... Page 185

# Quran Lessons Contents Page

| | |
|---|---|
| Lesson 7 - Quran …………………………………… | Page 17 |
| Lesson 14 - Quran …………………………………… | Page 31 |
| Lesson 21 - Quran …………………………………… | Page 47 |
| Lesson 28 - Quran …………………………………… | Page 61 |
| Lesson 35 - Quran …………………………………… | Page 75 |
| Lesson 43 - Quran …………………………………… | Page 91 |
| Lesson 49 - Quran …………………………………… | Page 103 |
| Lesson 56 - Quran …………………………………… | Page 117 |
| Lesson 63 - Quran …………………………………… | Page 131 |
| Lesson 70 - Quran …………………………………… | Page 145 |
| Lesson 77 - Quran …………………………………… | Page 159 |
| Lesson 84 - Quran …………………………………… | Page 173 |
| Lesson 91 - Quran …………………………………… | Page 187 |
| Lesson 98 - Quran …………………………………… | Page 201 |

*40 point font*

# Part A

REVIEW LESSONS

# Part A

Letters
Numbers
Colours
Spelling Numbers
Seasons
Days of the week
Months
Spacing

# LETTERS AND NUMBERS CHART

# LETTERS AND NUMBERS CHART

# LESSON 1 - REVIEW OF LETTERS

Write your name on the line below.

Carefully trace each letter and write the letter in the frame.

Aa　　　Bb　　　Cc　　　Dd

Ee　　　Ff　　　Gg　　　Hh

Ii　　　Jj　　　Kk　　　Ll

Mm　　　Nn　　　Oo　　　Pp

Draw a forest or a beach.

# LESSON 1 - REVIEW OF LETTERS

Colour all the capital letters red and the lowercase letters blue.

# LESSON 2 - REVIEW OF LETTERS

Write your name on the line below.

Carefully trace each letter and write the letter in the frame.

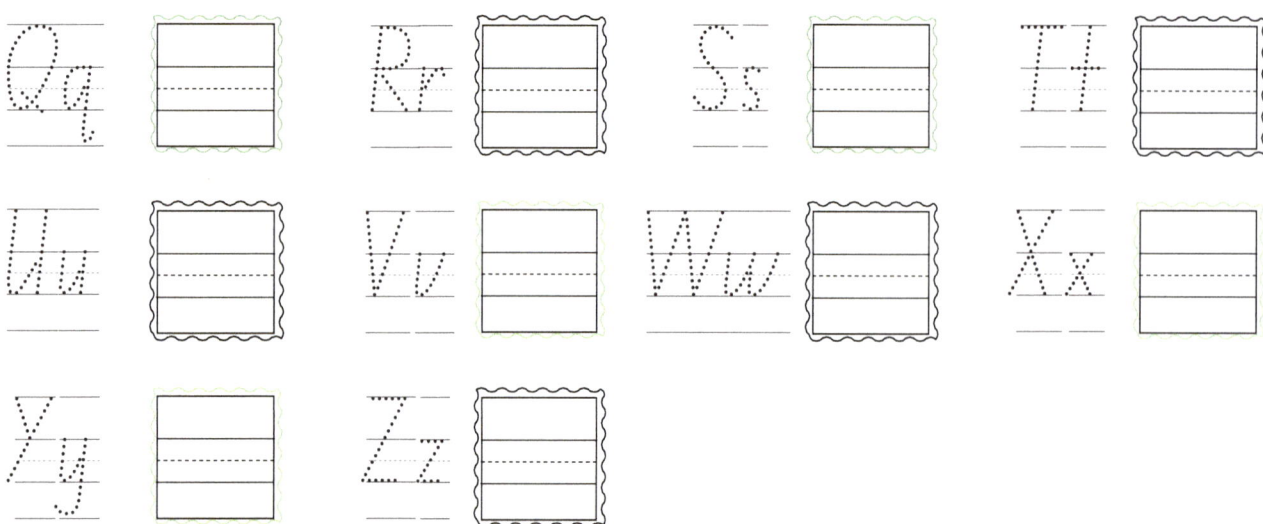

Colour the houses.

# LESSON 2 - REVIEW OF LETTERS

Colour all the capital letters red and the lowercase letters blue.

# LESSON 3 - REVIEW OF NUMBERS

Trace each number and write the number in the frame.

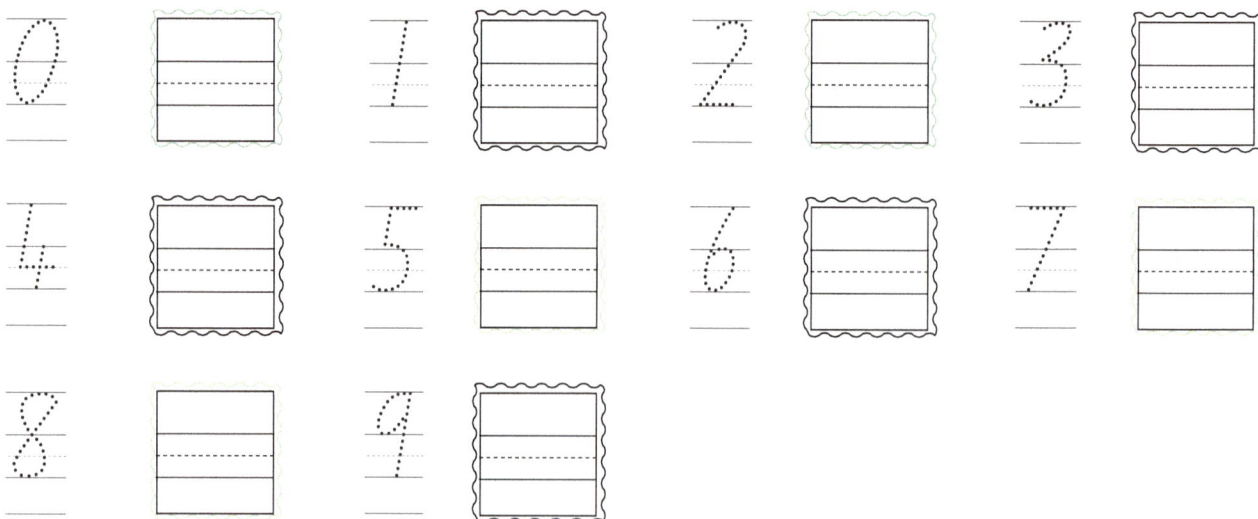

Number the first 3 Imams (as) and colour in their names.

Colour Imam Husain (as)'s shrine.

**Fun Fact :**
Imam Husain (as)'s shrine is located in Karbala, Iraq.

# LESSON 3 - REVIEW OF NUMBERS

Trace the numbers to fill in the blanks.

There is only 1 God.

He gave me 2 eyes.

I pray 5 times a day.

There are 12 Imams.

There are 114 surahs in the Quran.

Trace the numbers to fill in the blanks.  Colour the tasbeeh.

After we pray we say:

*Allahuakbar*
God is great.
Times

*Allhamdullilah*
Praise be to God.
Times

*Subhan Allah*
Glory be to God.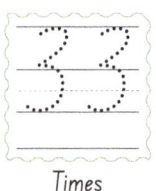
Times

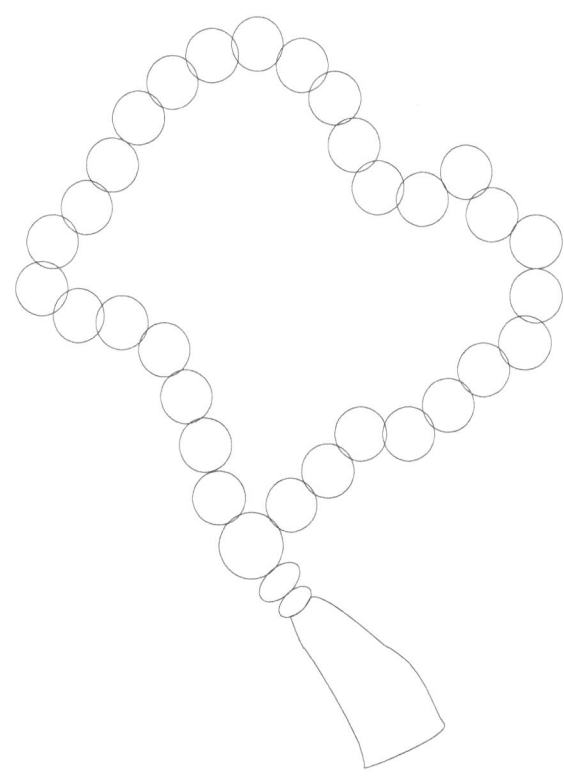

# LESSON 4 - REVIEW OF COLOURS

Trace the colours. In the boxes below draw something God has created in that colour.

# LESSON 4 - REVIEW OF COLOURS

Finish the sentence.

My favourite colour is _____.

Draw something God has created in your favourite colour.

Rainbow Writing: Write the words in their colour.

orange _____     red _____

yellow _____     blue _____

green _____     pink _____

# LESSON 5 - SPELLING NUMBERS

Look, trace and copy the numbers.

| One | One | ___ | 1 |
| Two | Two | ___ | 2 |
| Three | Three | ___ | 3 |
| Four | Four | ___ | 4 |
| Five | Five | ___ | 5 |

Colour the even numbers green and the odd numbers red.

# LESSON 5 - SPELLING NUMBERS

Look, trace and copy the numbers.

| Six   | Six   | _____ | 6  |
| Seven | Seven | _____ | 7  |
| Eight | Eight | _____ | 8  |
| Nine  | Nine  | _____ | 9  |
| Ten   | Ten   | _____ | 10 |

Colour the even numbers green and the odd numbers red.

# LESSON 6 - THE 12 IMAMS

Trace the names of the first six Imams.

Imam Ali (as)

Imam Hasan (as)

Imam Husain (as)

Imam Ali Zain al Abideen (as)

Imam Muhammad al Baqir (as)

Imam Jafar al Sadiq (as)

Copy the mosque in the blank box.

# LESSON 6 - THE 12 IMAMS

Trace the names of the last six Imams.

Imam Musa al Kadhim (as)

Imam Ali al Rida (as)

Imam Muhammad al Taqi (as)

Imam Ali al Hadi (as)

Imam Hasan al Askari (as)

Imam Muhammad Al Mahdi (ajtfs)

Copy the sentence.

We have twelve Imams.

## LESSON 7 - QURAN

So be quick to do good deeds

5:48

# LESSON 7 - QURAN

Trace the sentence.

*Make the right choices.*

Copy the sentences.

Do good.

Be kind.

Help others.

Have faith.

Colour the picture.

**Fun Fact :**
**There are 114 surahs in the Quran.**

# LESSON 8 - SEASONS

Copy the seasons.　　　　　　　　　　　　　　　　　Colour in the pictures.

Spring

Summer

Autumn

Winter

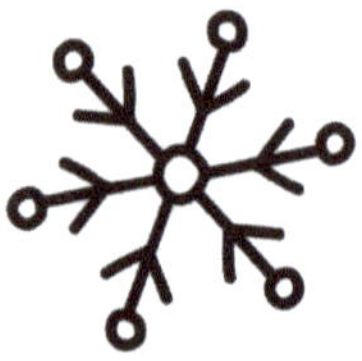

Draw a scene from your favourite season.

# LESSON 8 - SEASONS

Copy the sentence.

*Thank you God, for the seasons.*

Trace the words.

*flower*   *wind*   *sun*

*snow*   *leaf*   *tree*

Colour the pictures below.

# LESSON 9 - DAYS OF THE WEEK

Trace the days of the week.

*Monday*  *Tuesday*  *Wednesday*

*Thursday*  *Friday*  *Saturday*

*Sunday*

Colour the picture.

## LESSON 9 - DAYS OF THE WEEK

Trace and copy the sentence.

*I get better every single day.*

Copy each day of the week.

Monday

Tuesday

Wednesday

Thursday

Friday

Saturday

Sunday

# LESSON 10 - MONTHS

We have 12 months in a year, copy the names of the first 6 months.

*January*

*February*

*March*

*April*

*May*

*June*

Write the name of the month you were born in.

Write the name of the month we are in today.

# LESSON 10 - MONTHS

Copy the names of the last 6 months of the year.

July

August

September

October

November

December

Following the steps, draw the birthday cake in the blank box.

## LESSON 11 - MONTHS

Copy the poem on the lines below.

Thirty days in September,

April, June and November,

All the rest have thirty-one,

Except February alone,

And that has twenty-eight days clear,
And twenty-nine in each leap year.

# LESSON 11 - MONTHS

Trace the months with thirty days blue and thirty one days red.

January        Feburary        March

April        May        June        July

August        September        October

November        December

Colour the picture.

# LESSON 12 - PROPHET MUHAMMAD (PBUH)

Copy the sentence below.

## Prophet Muhammad (pbuh) is the last Prophet.

Prophet Muhammad (pbuh) was born in the Year of the Elephant. Colour in the elephant.

# LESSON 12 - PROPHET MUHAMMAD (PBUH)

Copy the sentence on the lines below.

*Prophet Muhammad (pbuh) was*

*truthful and trustworthy.*

Trace the sentences.

Colour Prophet Muhammads (pbuh) shrine.

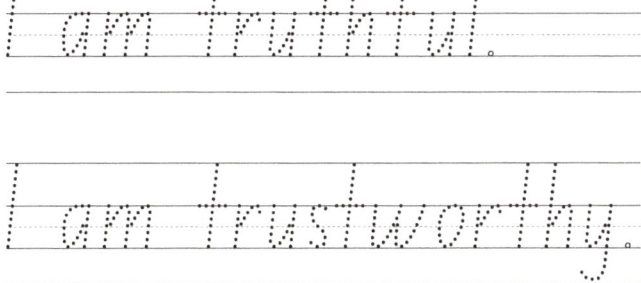

**Fun Fact :**
**Prophet Muhammads (pbuh) shrine is located in Medina.**

# LESSON 13 - SPACING

Remember to make sure that all letters are evenly spaced.

Be kind.  Be kind.
Correct   Incorrect

Look, trace and copy the sentences.

Be brave.

Be nice.

Be you.

Colour the picture,

# LESSON 13 - SPACING

Copy the sentences.

I love God.

God loves me.

Connect the dots and colour the heart.

## LESSON 14 - QURAN

And Allah loves those who are pure and clean

9:108

# LESSON 14 - QURAN

Trace and copy the sentence on the line below.

*I am going to shine today.*

Copy the sentences.

Smile often.

Speak nicely.

I am pure.

I am clean.

Colour the picture.

# LESSON 15 - SIMPLE SENTENCES

Trace and copy the sentences.

*Always say please.*

*Always say thank you.*

Draw a mountain under the goat.

# LESSON 15 - SIMPLE SENTENCES

Copy the sentence.

*Speak calmly and nicely.*

Copy the words on the lines below.

*calm*        *nice*        *polite*

Colour the picture.

## LESSON 16 - PART 1 REVIEW

Copy each letter once.

A B C D E F

G H I J K L

Write each number once.

1 2 3 4 5

Copy the colours.

red

orange

yellow

Colour the owl, then add the night sky, the moon and stars.

# LESSON 16 - PART 1 REVIEW

Copy each letter once.

a    b    c    d    e    f

g    h    i    j    k    l

Copy the first three days of the week.

Monday

Tuesday

Wednesday

Copy the first three months of the year.

January

Febuary

March

Draw a picture of anything you want to draw.

# LESSON 17 - PART 1 REVIEW

Copy each letter once.

N  O  P  Q  R  S

T  U  V  W  X  Y

Z  z

Copy each number once.

6   7   8   9   10

Copy the colours.                    Colour the picture.

green

blue

pink

# LESSON 17 – PART 1 REVIEW

Copy each letter once.

n  o  p  q  r  s

t  u  v  w  x  y

Copy the days of the week.

Thursday

Friday

Saturday

Copy the months.

April

May

June

Draw a face in each frame.

# LESSON 18 - LADY FATIMA (SA)

Copy the sentence on the line below.

Lady Fatima (sa) is the leader of the women of heaven.

Colour the picture.

# LESSON 18 - LADY FATIMA (SA)

Trace the sentence.

Lady Fatima (sa) is the daughter of Prophet Muhammad (pbuh) and the wife of Imam Ali (as).

Trace the sentences.

Draw flowers in the circles.

I am strong like Fatima.

I am brave like Fatima.

I am humble like Fatima.

I am modest like Fatima.

I am kind like Fatima.

I am pure like Fatima.

*33 point font*

# Part B

*Words and Sentences*

# Part B

*Tracing words and sentences.*

*Writing words and sentences.*

# LESSON 19

Trace and copy the sentences.

*God loves me.*

*I love God.*

Colour the boat, then add an ocean around it and draw yourself in it.

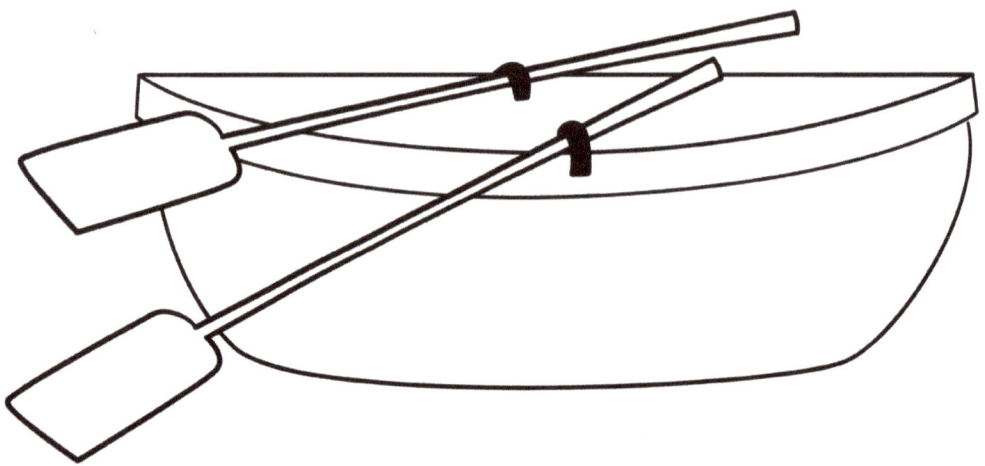

# LESSON 19

Trace the sentences.

Be kind.

Be nice.

Be patient.

Be honest.

Be grateful.

Colour the picture.

Draw a park in the box below.

# LESSON 20

Trace and copy the sentence on the line below.

*Never give up.*

Copy the sentences.

Work hard.

Help others.

Be grateful.

Be kind.

Colour the picture below.

# LESSON 20

Trace and copy the sentence on the line below.

*Be kind always!*

Copy the sentences.

Do good.

Be nice.

Smile often.

Dream big.

Draw a rainbow in the blank box.

## LESSON 21 - QURAN

# AND HELP ONE ANOTHER TO DO GOOD DEEDS

5:2

# LESSON 21 - QURAN

Trace and copy the sentence on the line below.

*Make the right choices.*

Copy the sentences.

Do good.

Help others.

Colour the picture below.

What good deed did you do today? Draw it in the box below.

# LESSON 22

Trace and copy the sentences.

*God loves me.*

*I love God.*

Colour the picture.

# LESSON 22

Trace and copy the sentences.

*I thank God for everything.*

*I share with others.*

Colour the picture.

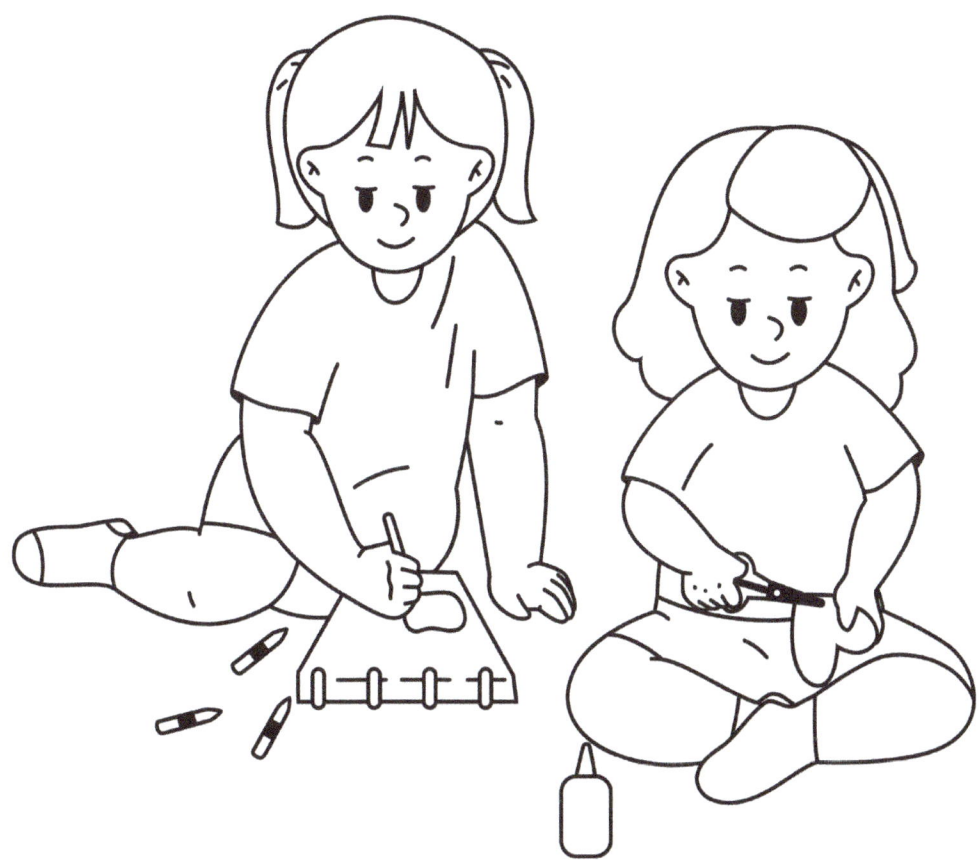

# LESSON 23

Copy the sentence on the line below.

*I love learning.*

Copy the names of the pets.

dog    cat    fish    bird

Draw your favourite animal from the list above.

# LESSON 23

Trace and copy the sentences.

*God loves me.*

*I am brave.*

Colour the picture.

# LESSON 24 - IMAM ALI (AS)

Copy the sentence on the line below.

Imam Ali (as) is the first Imam.

Trace the sentence.

Imam Ali (as) was the first and only person to be born in the Kaaba.

Colour in the Kaaba.

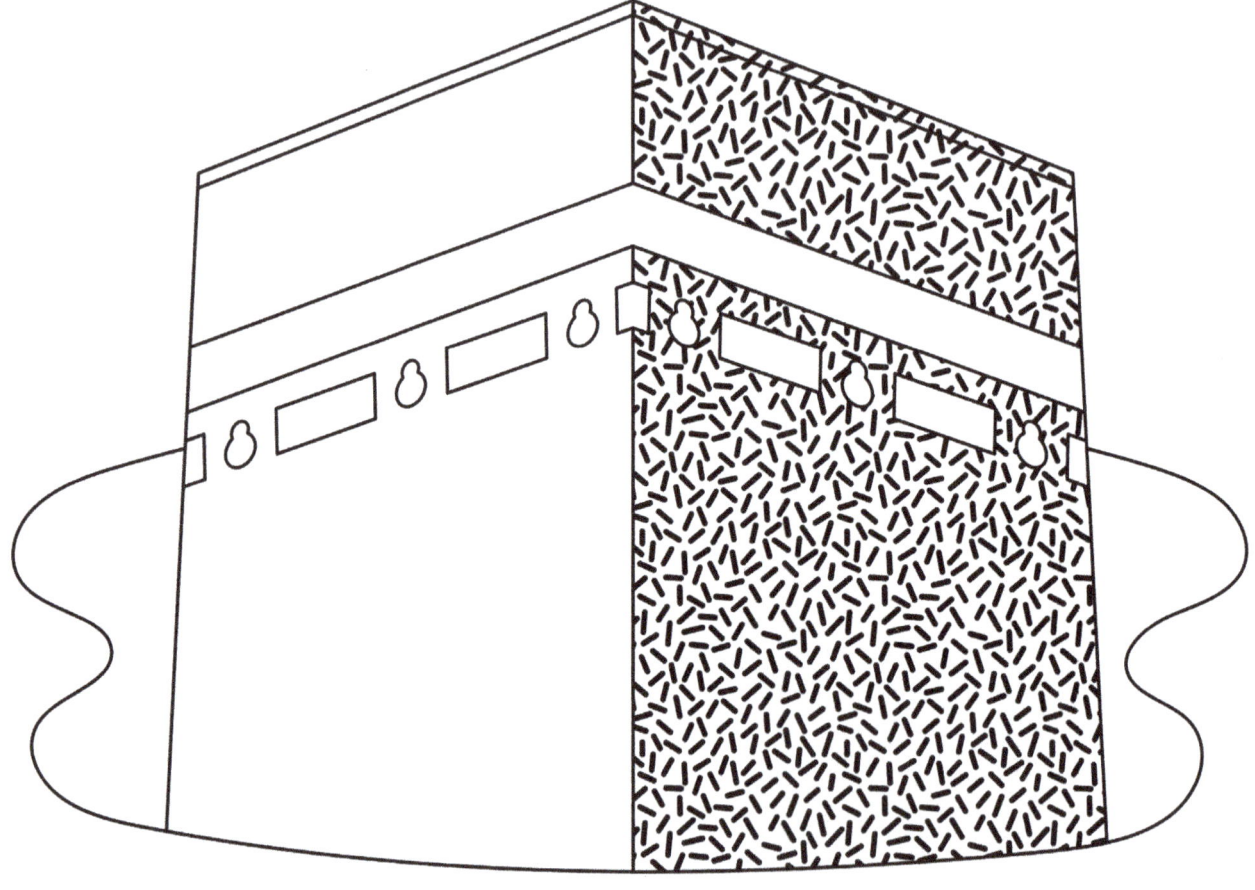

# LESSON 24 – IMAM ALI (AS)

Colour the different characteristics of Imam Ali (as).

Brave

Strong

Loyal

Humble

Charitable

Characteristics of Imam Ali (as)

Fed the poor

Loved to worship God

Took care of others

# LESSON 25

Copy the sentence on the line below.

*I can write neatly.*

Trace and copy the words.

rainy

windy

sunny

snowy

cloudy

foggy

Colour the image below.

Draw the weather outside today.

# LESSON 25

Trace the colours. Then in the boxes below draw an object in that colour.

*red*

*orange*

*yellow*

*green*

*blue*

*indigo*

# LESSON 26

Trace and copy the sentences.

*Always say please.*

*Always say thank you.*

Colour the picture.

# LESSON 26

Copy the sentence on the line below.

Do not waste.

Copy the words.

food

time

water

money

Draw your favourite food on the plate.

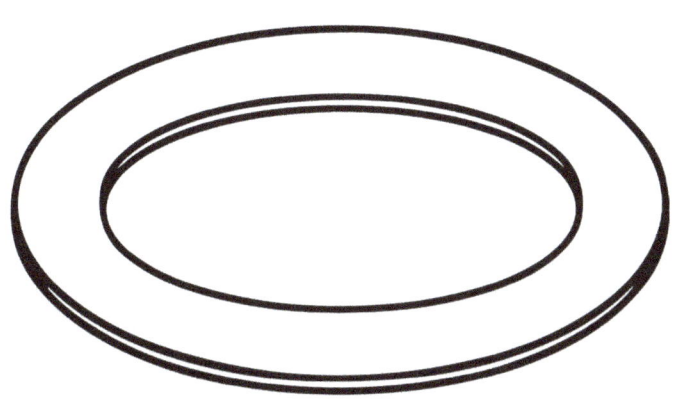

# LESSON 27

Trace the passage.

God made everything. He made the blue sky, the tall trees and the beautiful ocean.

Draw the scene described in the passage above.

# LESSON 27

Copy the sentences.

*Be kind and always do good.*

*Trust God with all your heart.*

*I am beautiful inside and out.*

Connect the dots and colour the picture.

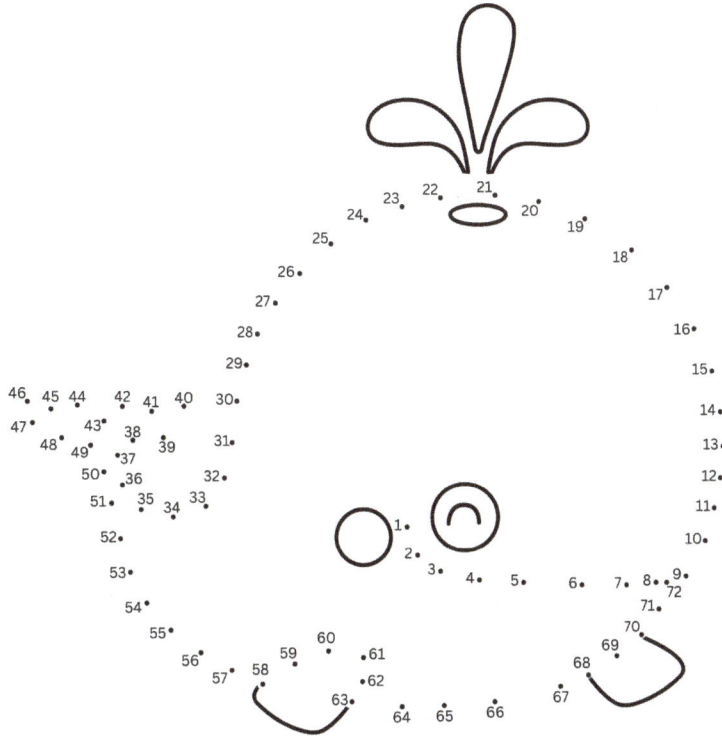

## LESSON 28 - QURAN

# BE GOOD TO YOUR PARENTS
## 17:23

# LESSON 28 - QURAN

Trace and copy the sentences.

*Be good to your parents.*

*Treat your parents with kindness.*

Copy each word twice.

kindness

parents

Draw a picture of you and your parents.

# LESSON 29

Copy the sentences.

*Love one another.*

*I put my trust in God.*

Trace the words.

*God*  *Love*  *Faith*  *Trust*

*God*  *Love*  *Faith*  *Trust*

Colour the picture.

## LESSON 29

Copy the sentences.

I will tell the truth.

I am a good listener.

Trace the sentences.

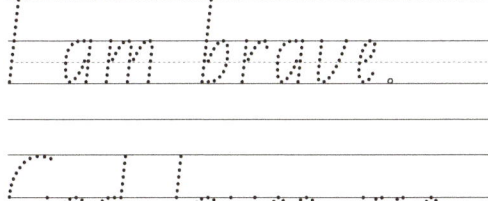

Colour the picture.

Draw the night sky.

# LESSON 30 - IMAM HASAN (AS)

Copy the sentence on the line below.

## Imam Hasan (as) is the second Imam.

Trace the sentence.

Imam Hasan (as) was the first son of Imam Ali and Lady Fatima (as). He was the first grandson of our Prophet Muhammad (pbuh). When he was born Prophet Muhammad (pbuh) named him Hasan and recited the athan in his right ear and the Iqama in his left ear.

**Fun Fact :**
Imam Hasan (as) and his brother Imam Husain (as) are the leaders of the youth of paradise.

# LESSON 30 - IMAM HASAN (AS)

Trace the quote from Imam Hasan (as) in any colour.

Treat others similar to the way you would like for them to treat you.

- Imam Hasan (as)

What act of kindness did you do today? Draw it in the box below.

Bihar-ul-Anwar, vol. 78, p. 116

# LESSON 31

Copy the sentences.

I love trees and nature.

I live in harmony with nature.

I will look after the Earth.

Copy the tree in the blank box.

# LESSON 31

Copy the sentences.

*I love learning.*

*I will always try my best!*

Trace the sentences.

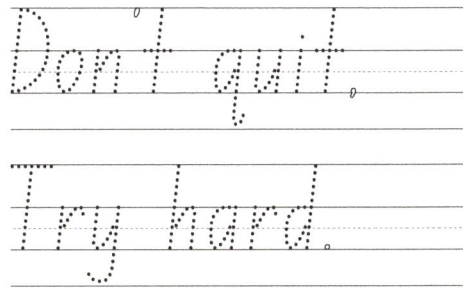

Colour the picture.

Draw a picture in the box below.

# LESSON 32

Trace the quote from Prophet Muhammad (pbuh) in your favourite colour.

*Every act of kindness is charity.*
*- Prophet Muhammad*
*(pbuh)*

Colour in the picture.

# LESSON 32

Trace and copy the sentence.

*Help others and give charity often.*

Copy the quote by Prophet Muhammad (pbuh) and colour the picture below.

Even a smile is charity.

# LESSON 33

Trace the sentences.

Draw a picture of yourself in the mirror.

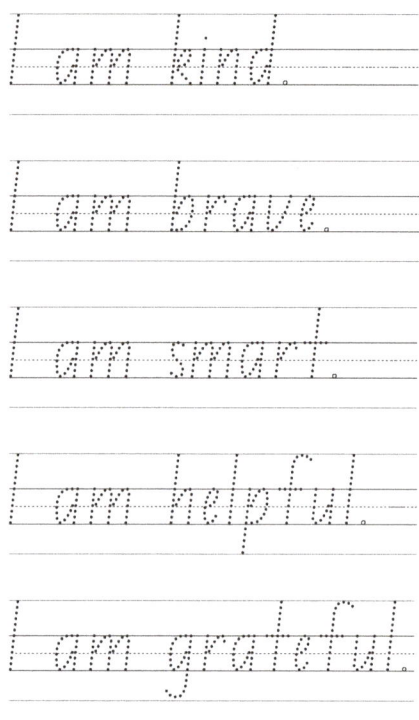

I am kind.
I am brave.
I am smart.
I am helpful.
I am grateful.

Colour the plane, and then draw a sky and some clouds.

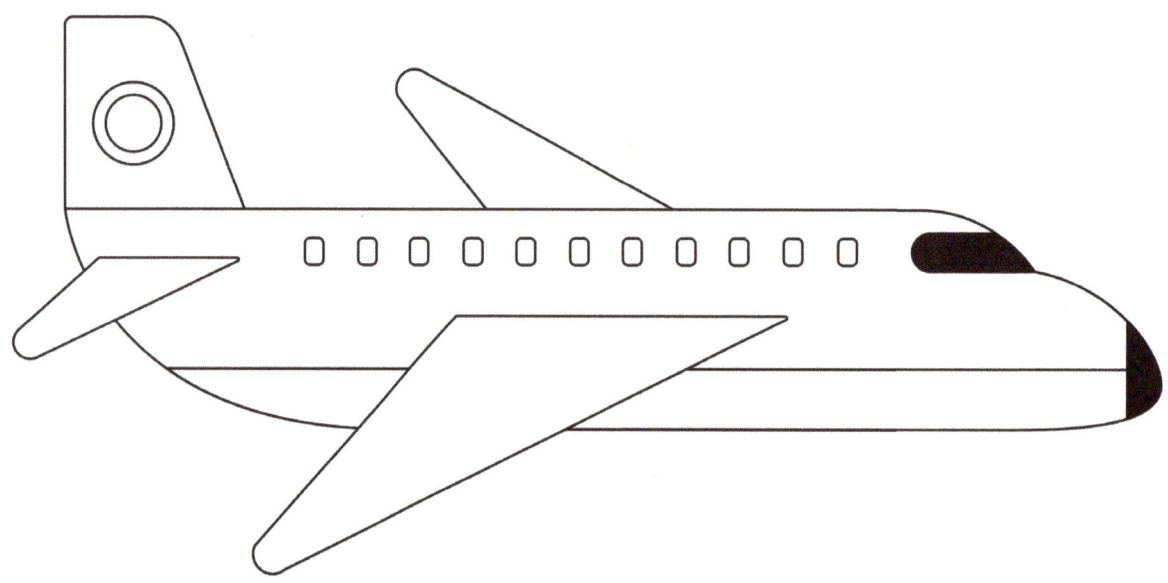

# LESSON 33

Trace and copy the sentences.

*I am proud of myself.*

*Mistakes help me learn and grow.*

Colour the picture.

# LESSON 34

Copy the sentences.

I am brave and strong.

I am smart and beautiful.

Trace the sentences.

I am enough.
I am strong.
I am unique.
I am loved.

Colour the picture.

Trace and copy the sentence.

I thank God for everything.

# LESSON 34

Trace and copy the sentences.

*I am confident and brave.*

*I am important and special.*

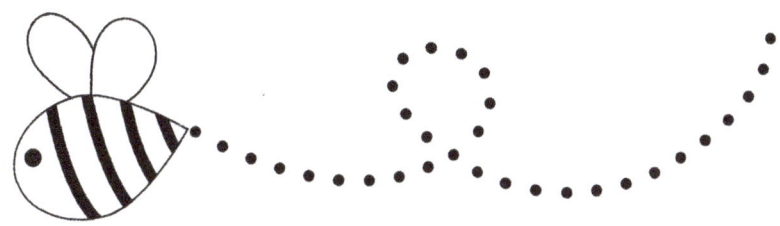

Copy the sentences.

*Be happy.*

*Be grateful.*

*Be you.*

Colour the picture.

## LESSON 35 - QURAN

# AND SPEAK TO PEOPLE NICELY

2:83

# LESSON 35 - QURAN

Copy each sentence twice.

I speak to others nicely.

I can brighten up anyones bad day.

Draw someone you love.

# LESSON 36 - IMAM HUSAIN (AS)

Copy the sentence on the line below.

## Imam Husain (as) is the third Imam.

Trace the sentence.

*Imam Husain (as) stood up to oppression.*

Colour the picture.

# LESSON 36 - IMAM HUSAIN (AS)

Copy the sentences.

I am brave like Imam Husain (as).

I am courageous like Imam Husain (as).

I am patient like Imam Husain (as).

I am forgiving like Imam Husain (as).

Draw something you are thankful for.

# LESSON 37

Copy the sentence on the line below.

*I love learning.*

Copy the names of the African animals.

lion    zebra    hippo

elephant    giraffe

Draw your favourite African animal from the list above.

# LESSON 37

Colour the sentence below.

*Pray and play every day!*

Trace and copy the sentences.

*Be kind to others.*

*Respect your parents.*

Colour the picture.

# LESSON 38

Copy the sentence.

*Think good thoughts.*

Copy the words on the lines below.

*love*  *joy*  *hope*

Copy the words.

*seed*

*leaf*

*green*

*grow*

Draw a picture using the words on the side.

# LESSON 38

Copy the sentence.

*Do good deeds.*

Copy the words on the lines below.

*love*  *trust*  *faith*

Copy the words.

*beach*

*coast*

*seaside*

*ocean*

Draw a picture using the words on the side.

# LESSON 39

Copy the sentences.

I am thankful for today.

I am grateful for today.

I will make the most of today.

Trace the words.

love

live

feel

life

Draw something you are grateful for today.

# LESSON 39

Copy the sentences.

*Today is going to be a great day.*

*I am feeling great today.*

Copy the words on the lines below.

*play*     *learn*     *grow*

Colour the picture.

# LESSON 40

Copy the sentence.

*Everything will be okay.*

Copy the words on the lines below.

*grateful*

*happy*

Trace the words.

*loved*   *loved*

*safe*   *safe*

*kind*   *kind*

Draw something big you saw today.

85

# LESSON 40

Copy the sentence.

*I can take deep breaths.*

*I am calm when things get hard.*

Copy the words.

*healthy*

*strong*

*honest*

*patient*

Colour the hot air balloon, then draw the sky, clouds and add some birds.

# LESSON 41

Trace and copy the sentences.

*God is the creator.*

*God is the most forgiving.*

Copy the words.

Colour the picture.

patient

humble

happy

# LESSON 41

Trace and copy the sentences. Then draw 4 family members in the circles.

*I go after my dreams.*

*I love my family and friends.*

○ ○ ○ ○

Copy the words.

*family*

*dreams*

*love*

Colour the picture.

# LESSON 42 - IMAM ALI ZAIN AL ABIDEEN (AS)

Copy the sentence on the line below.

## Imam Sajjad (as) is the fourth Imam.

Trace the sentences.

Imam Ali Zain al Abideen (as) was known as al Sajjad which means the worshipper of Allah (swt). He loved to pray and talked to Allah (swt) all the time.

Colour the picture of the man praying below.

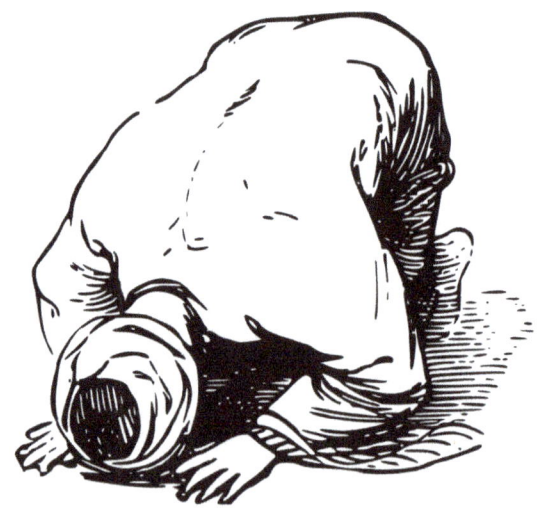

# LESSON 42 - IMAM ALI ZAIN AL ABIDEEN (AS)

Copy the sentences.

I love to pray.

I talk to God every day.

God is always with me, I am never alone.

Design your own prayer mat.

## LESSON 43 – QURAN

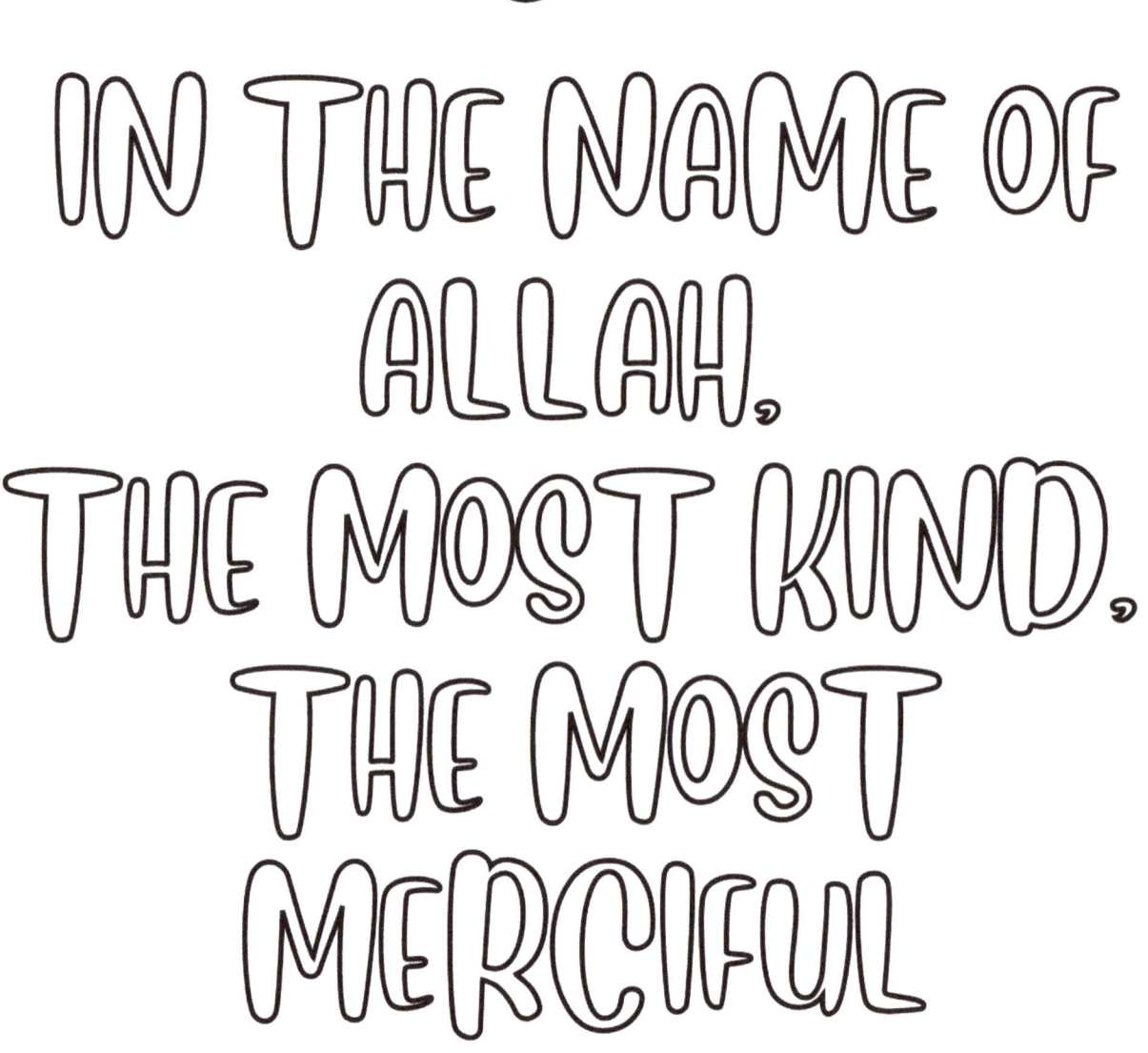

IN THE NAME OF ALLAH, THE MOST KIND, THE MOST MERCIFUL

1:1

# LESSON 43 - QURAN

Copy the sentences.

*Always say Bismillah before anything you do!*

*Always remember God.*

*God hears me when I pray.*

Colour the picture.

# LESSON 44

Trace and copy the sentences.

I love my Prophets.

I love my Imams.

Copy the words.

cuddle

giggle

cheerful

Colour the picture.

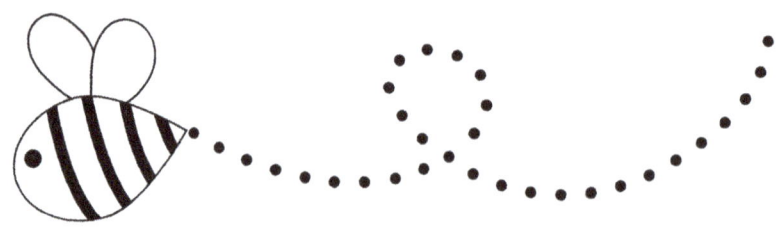

# LESSON 44

Copy the sentences.

*I am a reader.*

*I am a writer.*

*I am a storyteller.*

Draw a scene from your favourite book.

# LESSON 45

Trace and copy the sentences.

*God is great.*

*God is the most merciful.*

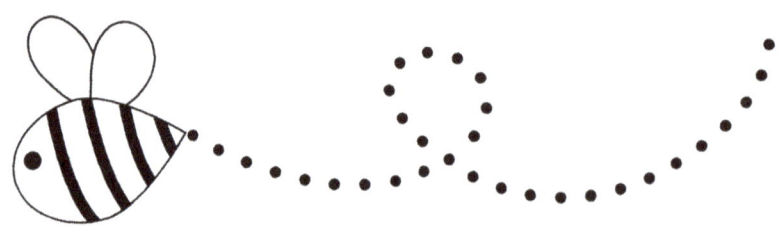

Copy the sentences.    Colour the picture.

Work hard.

Help others.

Smile often.

# LESSON 45

Copy the sentence.

I always do my best.

Copy the words.

shining.

joyful

amazing

loved

Draw something you love.

# LESSON 46

Copy the sentences.

I love God.

I love my Prophets.

I love my Imams.

Colour Prophet Noahs ark.

# LESSON 46

Copy the sentence.

*I will do great things today.*

*I will go after my dreams.*

Draw your future self.

# LESSON 47

Trace the sentence below.

*I have a brave heart and a brave soul.*

Copy the sentence.

*Have courage and be kind.*

Copy the words.

*brave*

*heart*

*brave*

*soul*

Colour the picture.

# LESSON 47

Copy the sentences.

God is the best protector.

God loves me.

Always remember God.

Draw a picture of anything you want.

# LESSON 48 - IMAM MUHAMMAD AL BAQIR (AS)

Copy the sentence on the line below.

## Imam Baqir (as) is the fifth Imam.

Trace the sentence.

*Imam Muhammad al Baqir (as) was known as al Baqir because of his tremendous knowledge.*

Colour the picture below.

# LESSON 48 - IMAM MUHAMMAD AL BAQIR (AS)

Copy the sentences.

I love to learn.

I learn something new every day.

Mistakes help me learn and grow.

Colour the picture below.

## LESSON 49 - QURAN

# ALLAH IS THE BEST PROTECTOR AND HE IS THE MOST MERCIFUL

12:64

# LESSON 49 - QURAN

Copy the sentences.

God is always with me, I am never alone.

God gives me strength.

I don't have to be afraid.

Look out your window and draw what you see.

# LESSON 50

Colour the sentence below.

## It is cool to be kind.

Trace the sentences.

I can brighten up anyones bad day.

Today is going to be a great day.

Copy the words.

loving

caring

friendly

Connect the dots and colour the picture.

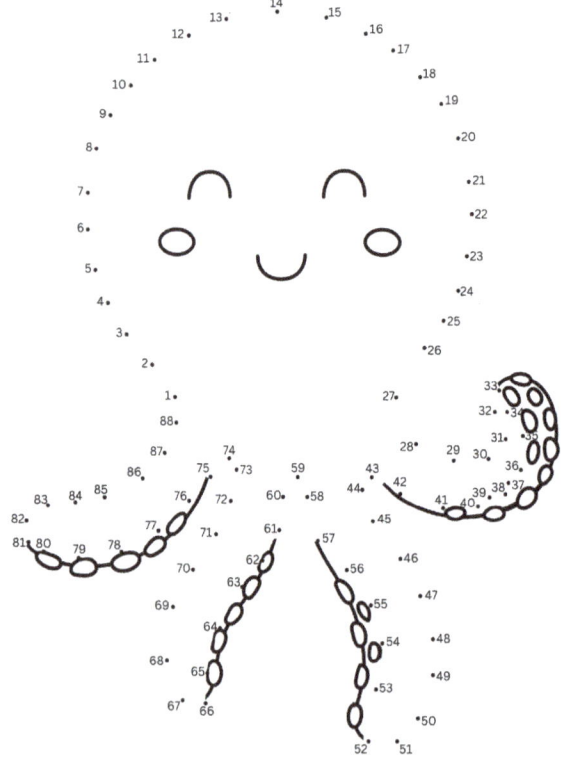

# LESSON 50

Copy the sentences.

*I love God.*

*I always thank God.*

*God is always with me.*

Trace the words.

*reading*   *playing*   *sleeping*

Colour the picture.

# LESSON 51

Copy the sentence.

*I can write neatly!*

Write your name on the line below.

Copy the words on the lines below.

*please*

*thank you*

Colour the picture below.

# LESSON 51

Copy the sentence.

*My writing is always neat.*

Inside the frames, write the 26 letters of the alphabet in capital letters.

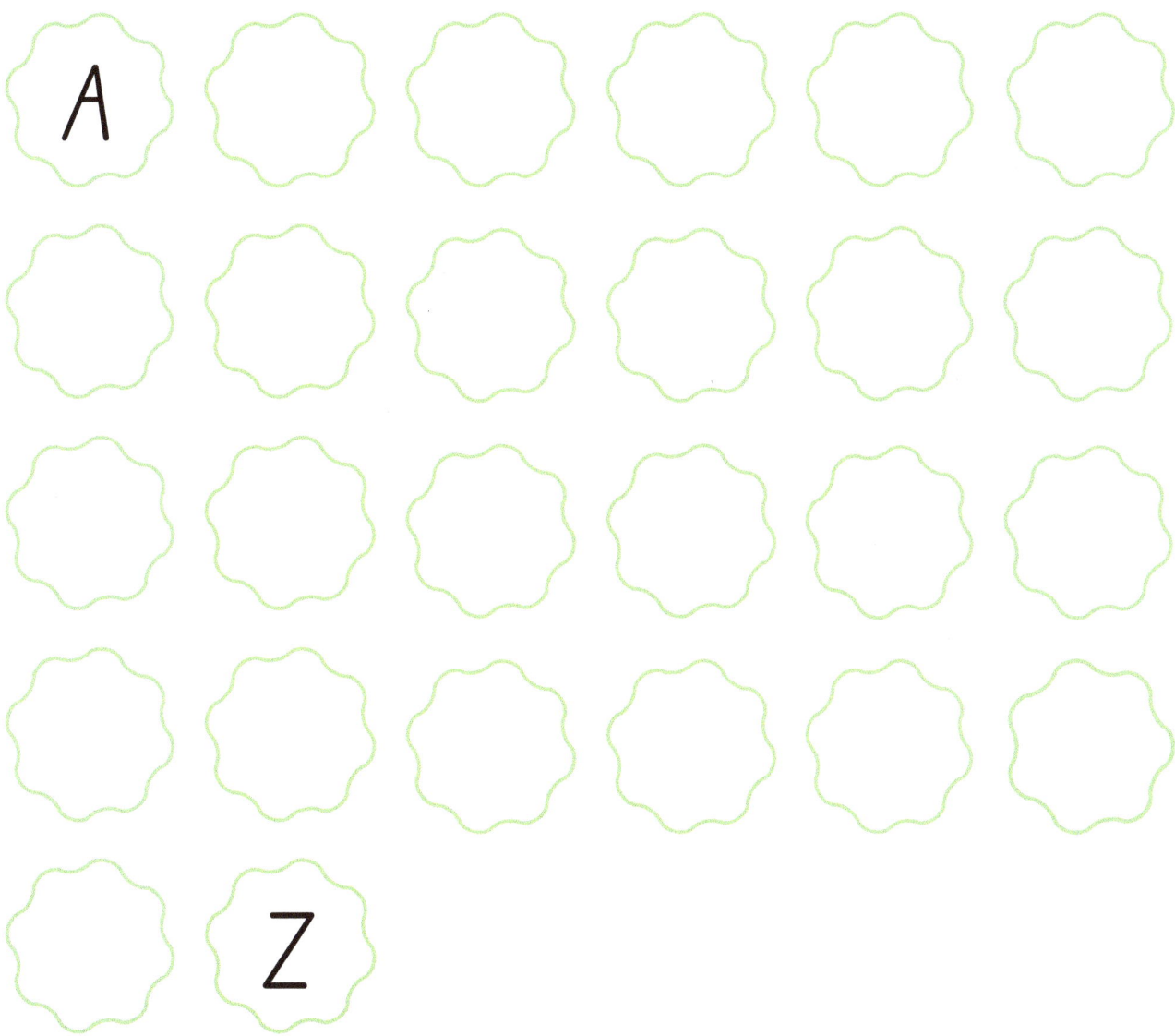

## LESSON 52

Copy the sentences.

*Trust God with all your heart.*

*God is always with me.*

Colour the picture.

# LESSON 52

Inside the clouds write the numbers from 1 to 10.

# LESSON 53

Copy the sentence.

*God is always with me.*

Copy the sentences on the lines below.

*Pray often*   *Smile often*   *Help others*

Colour the picture.

## LESSON 53

Copy the sentences.

*I can make the right choices.*

*I will do the right thing.*

Draw something you can see outside.

# LESSON 54 – IMAM JAFAR AL SADIQ (AS)

Copy the sentence on the line below.

Imam Jafar (as) is the sixth Imam.

Trace the sentence.

Imam Jafar (as) was known as al Sadiq
which means the truthful one.

Colour the picture below.

# LESSON 54 - IMAM JAFAR AL SADIQ (AS)

Copy the sentences.

I am truthful and trustworthy.

I am honest and kind.

Colour the quote below.

# HONESTY IS THE BEST POLICY

# LESSON 55

Copy the sentences.

*I put my trust in God.*

*I always thank God.*

Copy the words.

Draw a picture using the words on the side.

*flower*

*bee*

*grass*

*petals*

# LESSON 55

Copy the sentences.

I am beautiful inside and out.

I believe in myself.

Copy the sentences on the lines below.

Be kind.          Smile often.          Help others.

Colour the fox. Then draw a forest around him.

## LESSON 56 - QURAN

ASK ALLAH FOR FORGIVENESS
4:106

# LESSON 56 - QURAN

Copy the sentences.

God is forgiving. I can forgive others too.

I can be calm when things get hard.

I am kind to others.

Colour the picture.

# LESSON 57

Copy the sentences.

I can talk to God about anything.

God loves me.

Copy the words.

bird

nest

tree

eggs

Draw a picture using the words on the side.

# LESSON 57

Copy the sentences.

I am perfect just the way I am.

I love God.

Copy the words on the lines below.

care

share

fair

Copy the bee in the blank box.

# LESSON 58

Copy the sentences.

*Take care of the Earth.*

*Thank God for the Earth.*

Draw planet Earth.

# LESSON 58

Copy the sentences.

*God loves me and I love God.*

*God is with me wherever I am.*

Colour the picture.

# LESSON 59

Copy the sentences.

*God is the most forgiving.*

*I will set a good example.*

Draw apples on the tree and colour it in.

# LESSON 59

Copy the sentences.

*I can always improve.*

Copy the words on the lines below.

*prayer*          *patience*          *trust*

Colour the picture.

# LESSON 60 - IMAM MUSA AL KADHIM (AS)

Copy the sentence on the line below.

## Imam Musa (as) is the seventh Imam.

Trace the sentence.

Imam Musa (as) was known as al Kadhim which means the one who swallows his anger.

Colour the picture.

# LESSON 60 - IMAM MUSA AL KADHIM (AS)

Copy the sentences.

*I am patient like Imam Musa (as).*

*I am calm when things get hard.*

Draw a scene outside the window.

# LESSON 61

Copy the sentence on the lines below.

## Prophet Muhammad (pbuh) was

## truthful and trustworthy.

Trace the sentences.

Colour the picture.

Colour the picture.

# LESSON 61

Copy the sentence.

*I remember God as much as possible.*

Copy the words on the lines below.

*prayer*  *patience*  *trust*

Copy the sentences.

Draw the night sky in the window.

*Work hard.*

*Dream big.*

*Never give up.*

# LESSON 62

Copy the passage.

*God is always with me, he hears me and knows what is in my heart. I can talk to God about anything.*

Colour the whale. Then draw an ocean and some fish around it.

# LESSON 62

Write your name on the line below.

Copy the sentence.

*I remember God as much as possible.*

Draw a spider on the web.

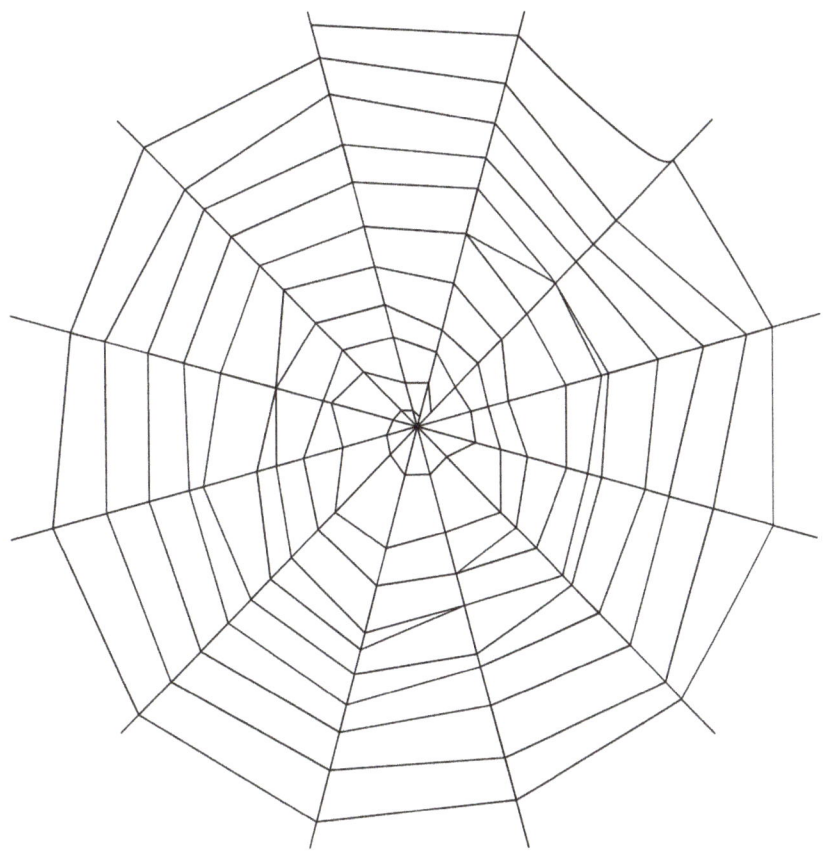

**Fun Fact :**
**The 29th Surah in the Quran is called the spider.**

## LESSON 63 - QURAN

# MY LORD INCREASE MY KNOWLEDGE

20:114

## LESSON 63 - QURAN

Copy the sentences.

*I am excited to learn new things today.*

*It is okay to ask for help.*

Trace the sentence.

*I am capable of being great and hard working.*

Draw some books on the shelf.

# LESSON 64

Copy the sentences.

*I put my trust in God.*

*I am going to have a great day.*

Colour the picture.

# LESSON 64

Copy the sentences.

*I am patient when things get hard.*

*I can get through anything.*

Trace the sentences.

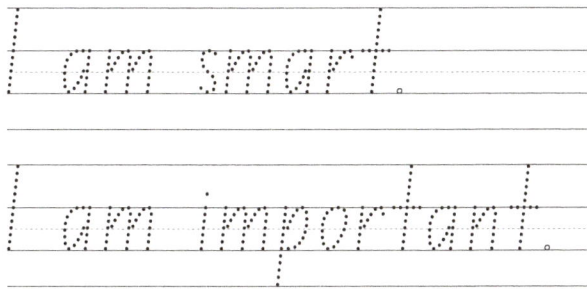

Colour the picture.

Draw a picture of anything you want.

# LESSON 65

Copy the sentence on the line below.

*I love learning.*

Copy the names of the sea animals.

fish        shark        whale

crab        turtle        sea horse

Draw your favourite sea animal from the list above.

# LESSON 65

Copy the sentence.

*I can write neatly.*

Inside the frames, write the 26 letters of the alphabet in lowercase letters.

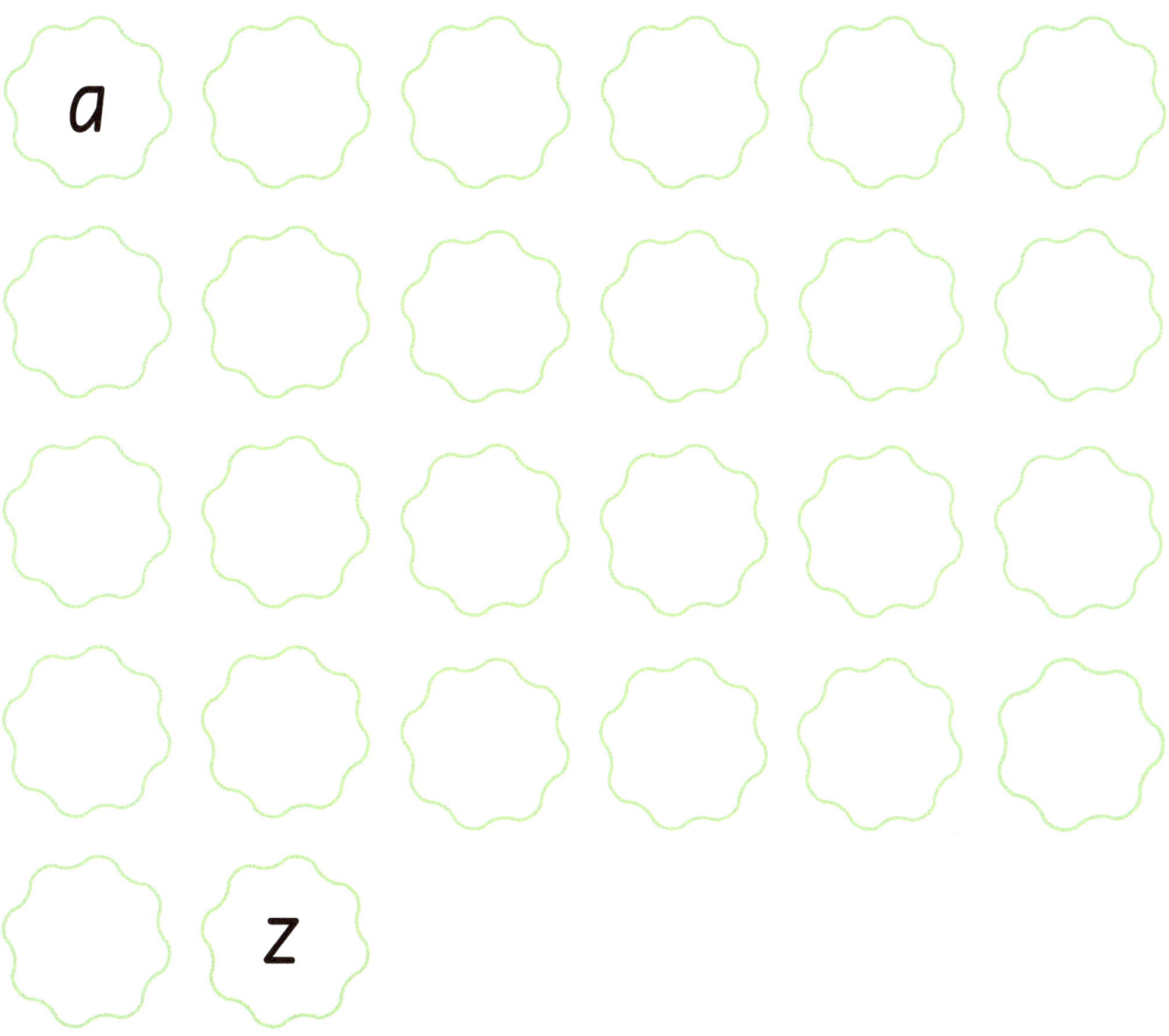

# LESSON 66 - IMAM ALI AL RIDA (AS)

Copy the sentence on the line below.

Imam Rida (as) is the eighth Imam.

Trace the sentence.

Imam Ali al Rida (as) was known as the grateful one.

Draw something you are grateful for.

# LESSON 66 - IMAM ALI AL RIDA (AS)

Copy the sentences.

I am grateful like Imam Ali al Rida (as).

I thank God for everything.

God has given me so many blessings.

Draw something God has blessed you with.

# LESSON 67

Copy the sentences.

*God has a purpose for my life.*

*God loves me and I love God.*

Draw a heart in the box below.

# LESSON 67

Copy the sentences.

*I can always find comfort in God.*

*God is greater than the world.*

Colour the picture.

# LESSON 68

Trace and copy the sentence.

*There is no God but Allah (swt) and Muhammad (pbuh) is his messenger.*

Connect the dots and colour the picture.

# LESSON 68

Copy the sentences.

God is the most gracious.

God is the most merciful.

God is always with us.

Colour the picture.

# LESSON 69

Trace and copy the sentence.

*Prophet Muhammad (pbuh) was born in the year of the elephant.*

Connect the dots and colour the picture.

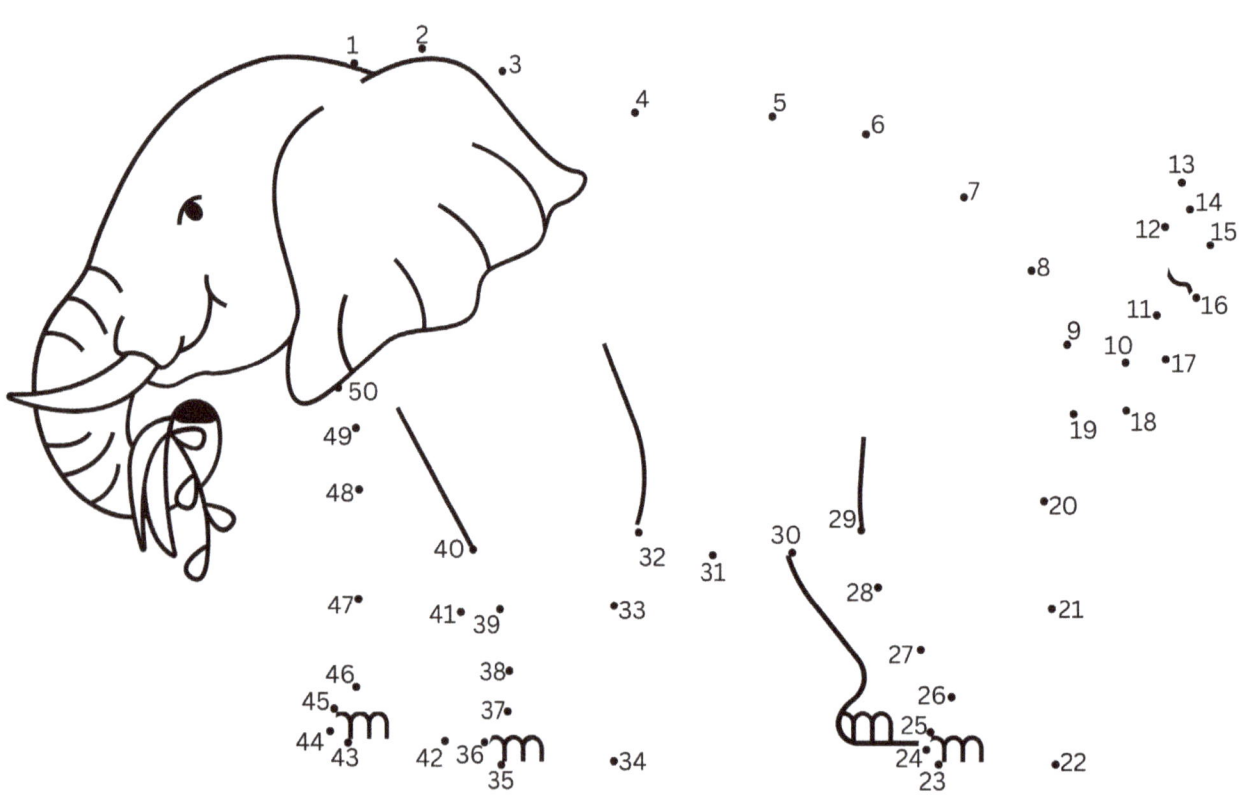

# LESSON 69

Copy the sentences.

Always remember God.

God is the All Knowing.

There is no one like him.

Draw something you can see outside.

## LESSON 70 - QURAN

# BE GRATEFUL TO ALLAH

31:12

## LESSON 70 - QURAN

Copy the sentences.

I am grateful for everything.

God has given me so many blessings.

I thank God for everything.

Draw something you are grateful for.

# LESSON 71

Colour the sentence below.

## Follow your dreams.

Trace the sentences.

*I can brighten up anyones bad day.*

*Today is going to be a great day.*

Copy the words.

braver

stronger

smarter

Colour the picture.

# LESSON 71

Copy the sentences.

I thank God for everything.

God loves me.

I love God.

Colour the turtle. Then draw the ocean and some fish around it.

# LESSON 72 - IMAM MUHAMMAD AL TAQI (AS)

Copy the sentence on the line below.

Imam Taqi (as) is the ninth Imam.

Trace the sentence.

Imam Muhammad al Taqi (as) was known

as the generous one.

Draw a picture of you helping others.

# LESSON 72 - IMAM MUHAMMAD AL TAQI (AS)

Copy the sentences.

I am kind to those around me.

I love helping others.

I give to the needy.

Colour the picture below.

# LESSON 73

Copy the sentence.

*I am beautiful inside and out.*

Write the country and state that you live in.

Copy the words on the lines below.

*please*    *thank you*

Colour the animals.

# LESSON 73

Copy the sentences.

God sees the good deeds that I do.

I am proud of myself.

Trace the sentences.

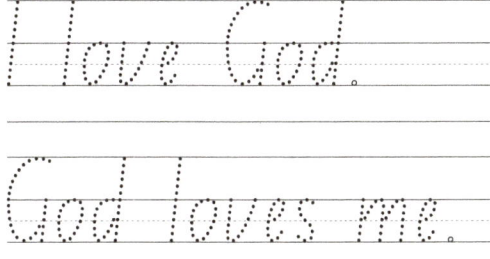

Colour the picture.

What good deed did you do today? Draw a picture below.

# LESSON 74

Copy the sentences.

God helps me do hard things.

I can talk to God about anything.

Colour the picture.

# LESSON 74

Copy the sentences.

God loves me.

God is always with me.

God gives me strength.

Colour the picture.

# LESSON 75

Copy the sentences.

*God created everything.*

*God is always with me.*

Copy the words.

*sun*

*moon*

*clouds*

*stars*

Draw a picture using the words on the side.

# LESSON 75

Copy the sentences.

*God created the sun and the moon.*

*God created the clouds and the stars.*

Colour the picture.

# LESSON 76

Copy the sentences.

I am perfect just the way I am.

I believe in myself.

Trace the sentences.

Be brave.

Be kind.

Be creative.

Be thankful.

Be happy.

Be you.

Colour the picture.

## LESSON 76

Copy the passage.

*You are braver than you believe. Stronger than you seem. Smarter than you think, and loved more than you know.*

Colour the picture.

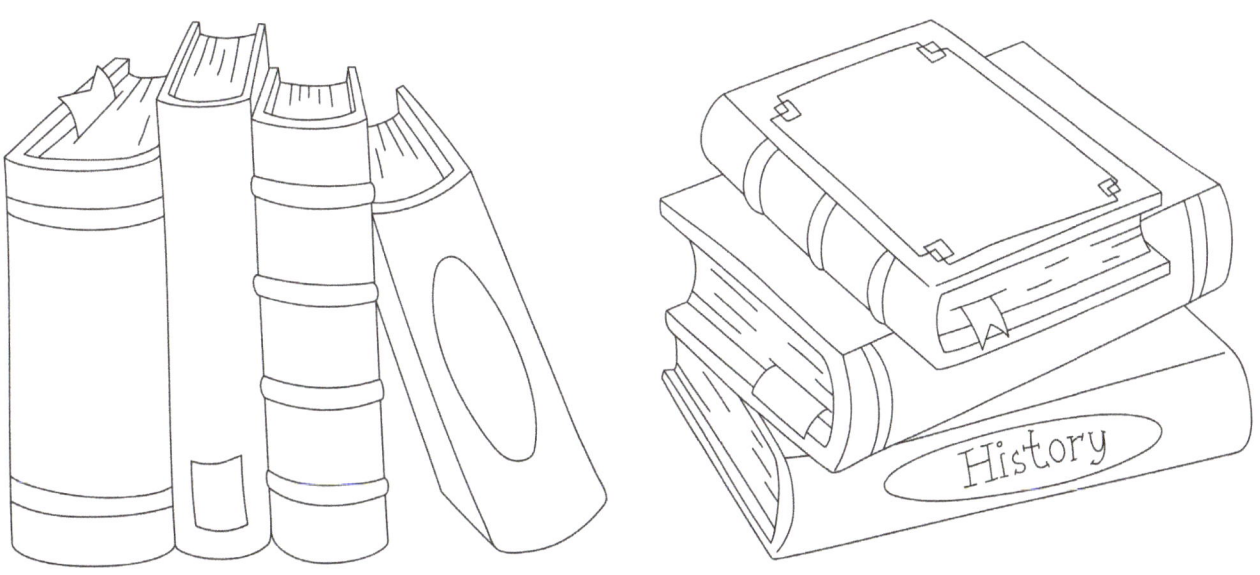

## LESSON 77 - QURAN

# HAVE PATIENCE

11:115

# LESSON 77 - QURAN

Copy the sentences.

*I am patient when things get hard.*

*I can get through anything.*

Colour the picture.

# LESSON 78 - IMAM ALI AL HADI (AS)

Copy the sentence on the line below.

## Imam Hadi (as) is the tenth Imam.

Trace the sentence.

*Imam Ali al Hadi (as) was known as the guide and the pure one.*

Colour the picture.

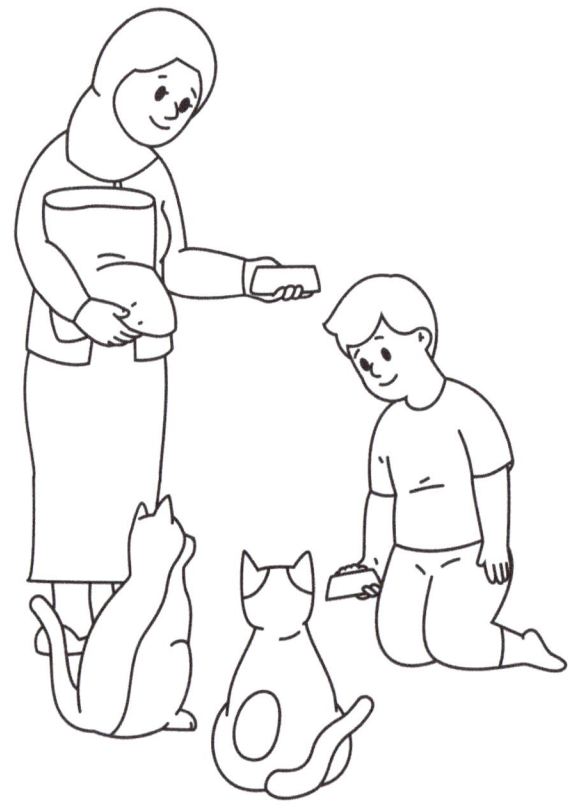

# LESSON 78 - IMAM ALI AL HADI (AS)

Copy the sentences.

*I am pure like Imam Ali al Hadi.*

*I am gentle and kind.*

Colour the picture.

# LESSON 79

Trace and copy the sentence.

*A noun is a word that names a person, place or thing.*

Copy the nouns.

*dad*    *home*    *hat*

Draw a picture of one of the nouns above.

# LESSON 79

Copy the sentence.

*Speak calmly and nicely.*

Copy the words on the lines below.

*calm*  *nice*  *polite*

Colour the picture.

## LESSON 80

Copy the sentences.

*I am respectful and kind.*

*I am grateful for everything.*

Draw something that you are grateful for.

# LESSON 80

Copy the sentence.

*Dear God, please bless my home.*

Copy the sentences on the lines below.

*Have faith.*   *Be honest.*   *Be kind.*

Draw your home.

# LESSON 81

Copy the sentence on the line below.

*I love learning.*

Copy the names of the farm animals.

cow           duck           sheep

horse         chicken        pig

Draw your favourite farm animal from the list above.

# LESSON 81

Copy the sentences.

*Everything happens for a reason.*

*I put my trust in God.*

Connect the dots and colour the picture.

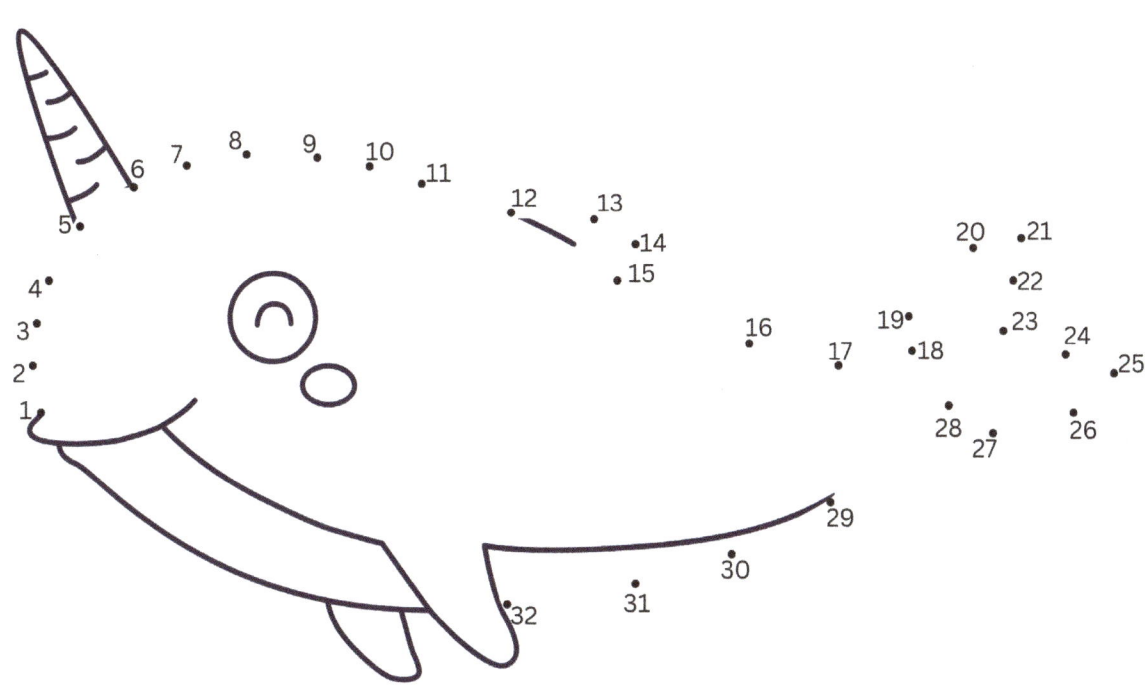

# LESSON 82

Copy the sentence on the line below.

*I am thankful for today.*

Copy the words on the lines below.

*love*  *live*  *life*

Draw something you are thankful for.

# LESSON 82

Copy the sentence.

*I am loved by God, my parents, my family and my friends.*

Copy the words.

*mindful*

*joyful*

*happy*

*clever*

Colour the picture.

# LESSON 83

Copy the sentence on the line below.

I love God.

Write 4 words that describe Prophet Muhammad (pbuh).

Colour the picture.

# LESSON 83

Copy the words.

*brown*                *black*                *white*

Copy the words on the lines below.

*plant*                *tree*                 *shell*

Draw a plant, a tree or a shell.

## LESSON 84 - QURAN

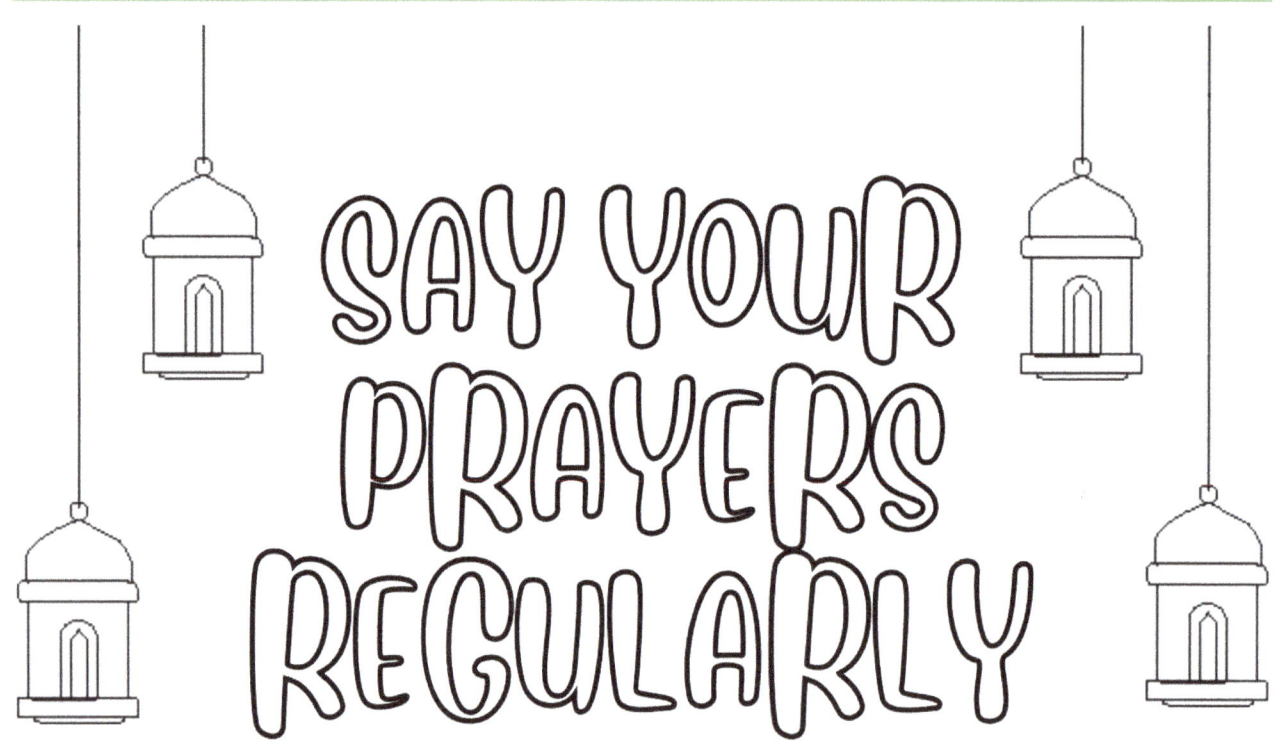

31:17

# LESSON 84 - QURAN

Copy the sentences.

I pray five times a day.

God hears me when I speak to him.

I can talk to God about anything.

Colour the prayer mat.

# LESSON 85 - IMAM HASAN AL ASKARI (AS)

Copy the sentence on the line below.

## Imam Askari (as) is the eleventh Imam.

Trace the sentence.

*Imam Hasan al Askari (as) was known as the soldier of God.*

Colour the clouds with the number eleven.

# LESSON 85 - IMAM HASAN AL ASKARI (AS)

Copy the sentences.

I am kind and generous.

I am patient and forgiving.

I am truthful and trustworthy.

Colour the picture.

## LESSON 86

Copy the sentences.

*Before we eat we say Bismillah.*

*Before we sleep we say Alhamdulilah.*

Colour the picture.

# LESSON 86

Copy the sentence.

*Every problem has a solution.*

Copy the words on the lines below.

*sand*　　　*bush*　　　*flowers*

Colour the picture.

# LESSON 87

Trace and copy the sentence.

*A noun is a word that names a person,*

*place or thing.*

Copy the nouns.

mum        chair        park

Draw a picture of one of the nouns above.

# LESSON 87

Copy the sentence.

*Today I will be the best version of me.*

Draw a picture of yourself in the mirror.

# LESSON 88

Copy the sentence.

Love one another.

Copy the words on the lines below.

pot　　　　plant　　　　leaf

Draw a picture using the words above.

# LESSON 88

Copy the poem.

The sun is shining,
The sky is blue,
The birds are flying,
The day is new.

Draw a picture inspired by the poem.

# LESSON 89

Copy the sentences.

## If I fall, I will get back up again.

## My mistakes help me learn and grow.

Colour the picture.

# LESSON 89

Write your name on the line below.

Copy the sentence.

*Today I will be the best version of me.*

Trace the sentences.

*Be brave.*

*Be kind.*

*Be creative.*

*Be thankful.*

*Be happy.*

*Be you.*

Colour the picture.

# LESSON 90 - IMAM MAHDI (AJTFS)

Copy the sentence on the line below.

## Imam Mahdi (ajtfs) is the twelfth Imam.

Trace the sentence and colour the picture.

*Imam Muhammad al Mahdi (ajtfs) is the last Imam.*

Copy the sentences.

## I am courageous and confident.

## I am patient and forgiving.

## Today I will be the best version of me.

# LESSON 90 - IMAM MAHDI (AJTFS)

## LESSON 91 - QURAN

# AND MAKING PEACE IS BETTER

4:128

# LESSON 91 - QURAN

Copy the sentences.

I am kind to others.

I am a good listener.

Every problem has a solution.

Connect the dots and colour the picture.

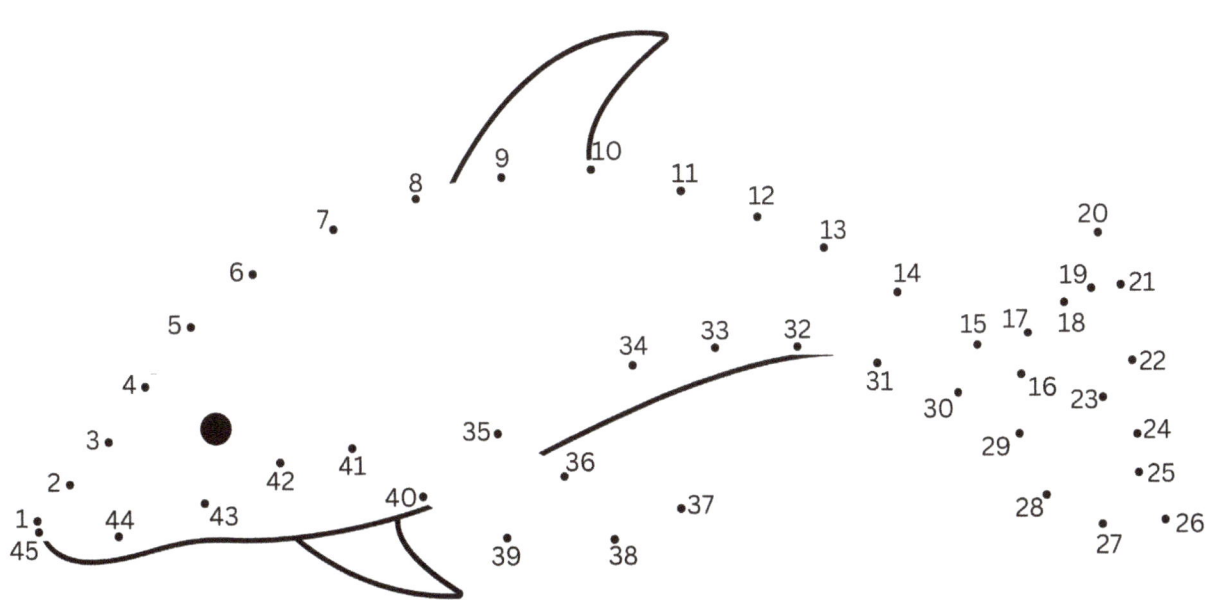

# LESSON 92

Copy the sentences.

God is always with me.

I love God with all my heart.

Colour the picture.

# LESSON 92

Copy the sentences.

Love one another.

I love my family.

Draw someone that you love and are grateful for.

# LESSON 93

Copy the sentences.

God helps me do hard things.

I can talk to God about anything.

Colour the picture.

# LESSON 93

Trace the sentence.

*There is no God but Allah (swt)*

*and Muhammad (pbuh) is his messenger.*

Colour the picture.

# LESSON 94

Trace a part of Imam Sajjads (as) morning supplication.

*Praise belongs to God,*

*who created night and day*

*through His strength*

*and set them apart*

*through His power.*

Colour the picture.

# LESSON 94

Copy the sentences.

I am brave and strong.

I am smart and beautiful.

I am a Muslim.

Colour the picture.

# LESSON 95

Trace and copy the sentence.

*A noun is a word that names a person, place or thing.*

Copy the words.

*dad*   *mum*   *brother*   *sister*

Draw a picture of your family sitting on the couch.

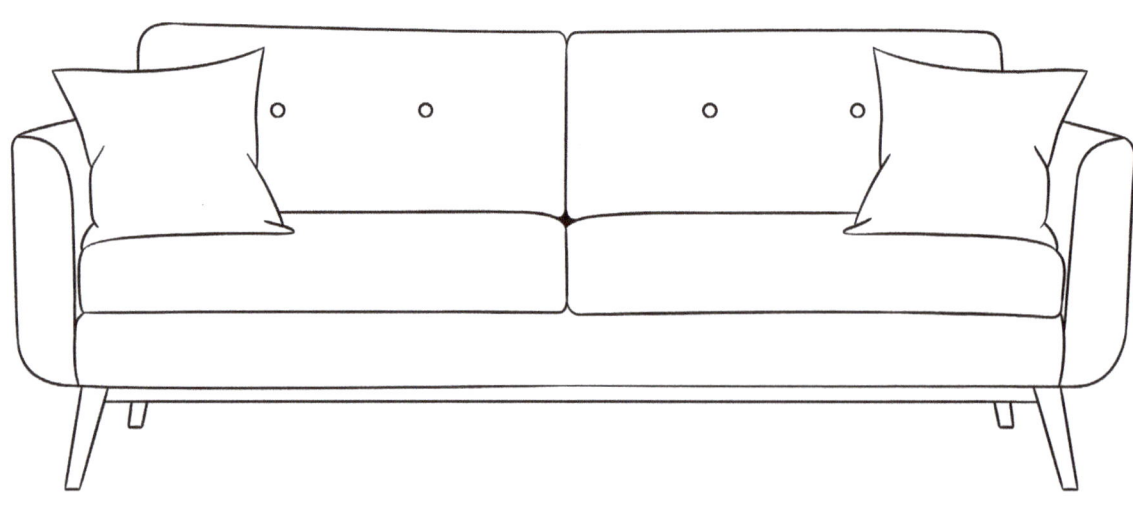

# LESSON 95

Trace the sentence.

*God is always with me.*

Copy the sentences.

Love God.

Trust God.

Seek God.

Ask God.

Praise God.

Thank God.

Colour the pictures.

# LESSON 96

Trace the I am Thankful poem.

I am Thankful...

For flowers and squirrels and birds that have wings.

For lions and tigers and all living things.

For mountains and rivers, for water and air.

For Mum and Dad who show me they care.

For food on my table, and something to drink.

For yellow, orange, purple and pink.

## LESSON 96

Copy the sentences.

*Start your day with Bismillah.*

*End your day with Alhamdulilah.*

Draw a sunrise or a sunset.

# LESSON 97

Copy the sentences.

God gives me strength.

God gives me peace.

God protects me.

Colour the picture.

# LESSON 97

Copy the sentences.

*I am an amazing person.*

*I am going to shine today.*

Colour the picture.

## LESSON 98 - QURAN

# Do Good.
# Allah Loves The
# Doers of Good

2:195

# LESSON 98 - QURAN

Copy the sentences.

Do good.

Be kind.

Help others.

Have faith.

What good did you do today?

Draw a picture to match the sentence you wrote above.

# LESSON 99

Copy the sentences.

Treat your parents with respect.

Treat your parents with kindness.

Treat your parents with care.

Draw a picture of you and your parents.

# LESSON 99

Copy the sentences.

*I am grateful for my parents.*

*I am grateful for my family.*

*I am grateful for my home.*

Colour the picture.

# LESSON 100

Colour the sentence below.

## Be truthful and avoid telling lies.

Trace the sentence.

*Prophet Muhammad was truthful and trustworthy.*

Copy the words.

Truthful

Trustworthy

Patient

Colour the picture.

# LESSON 100

Copy the sentences.

I ask for forgiveness.

God is the most forgiving.

God is the most merciful.

Draw the sun and some rain, then colour in the rainbow.

# LESSON 101

Copy the sentences.

*Earth is a blessing from God.*

*I will take care of the Earth.*

Draw a save planet Earth poster.

# LESSON 101

Copy the sentences.

We should not waste food and water.

We should throw our rubbish in the bin.

We should be kind to the Earth.

Colour in the picture.

# LESSON 102

Trace and copy the sentence.

*God is the most kind, the most merciful.*

*God is forgiving and I can forgive others*

*too.*

Copy the words.

*kind*    *mercy*    *forgive*

Draw something that you love.

# LESSON 102

Copy the sentences.

*I can be calm when I am upset.*

*The challenges I face make me strong.*

Copy the words.

*calm*   *strong*   *patient*

Colour the picture.

# LESSON 103

Trace the sentences.

*I am brave and confident.*

*I follow my dreams.*

Copy the words.

*brave*      *confident*      *loved*

Following the steps, draw the strawberry in the blank box.

## LESSON 103

Copy the sentence.

*I have the power to make my dreams come true.*

Colour in the quote.

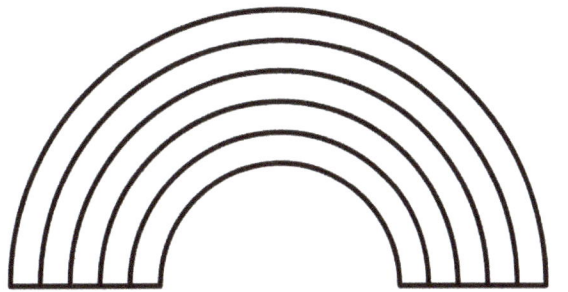

# LESSON 104

Copy the sentences.

*I can make a difference in this world.*

*I believe in myself and what I can do.*

Colour the pictures.

## LESSON 104

Copy the sentence.

*I am a good role model for those who are younger than me.*

Draw your future self.

www.ingramcontent.com/pod-product-compliance
Lightning Source LLC
Chambersburg PA
CBHW042021090526
44591CB00024B/2924